Britton Finds a Kitten

By Kari Capone
Illustrated by Yu-Mei Han

Scott Foresman
is an imprint of

Glenview, Illinois • Boston, Massachusetts • Chandler, Arizona •
Upper Saddle River, New Jersey

Illustrations
Yu-Mei Han.

Photographs

Every effort has been made to secure permission and provide appropriate credit for photographic material. The publisher deeply regrets any omission and pledges to correct errors called to its attention in subsequent editions.

Unless otherwise acknowledged, all photographs are the property of Pearson Education, Inc.

16 Fema/Getty Images.

ISBN 13: 978-0-328-50755-9
ISBN 10:   0-328-50755-5

9 10 11 V010 17 16 15 14 13

"Dad, look!" called Britton.

He crouched on the sidewalk and peeked under a car. A tiny animal with orange and white fur peeked at Britton.

"It's a kitten!" said Britton. "Can we keep it?"

"Yes," said Dad. "The kitten will need a bed and some food."

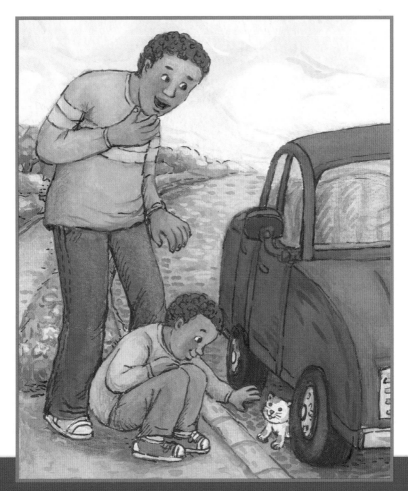

Britton found an empty shoebox in his closet. "This will make a good bed," he thought. He found a pillowcase to make the bed soft.

Britton found a can of tuna fish in the kitchen. "Kittens love tuna fish," he thought.

Britton took the food and bed to Dad.

Dad smiled at Britton. "That is a good bed," he said. "This is a very small kitten. She can eat tuna fish when she is more mature. We will buy kitten food at the pet store."

Britton and Dad went to the pet store. They asked the owner for help. They found food and milk for the kitten. They also found toys for the kitten.

"Next we will visit the vet," said
Dad.

"What is a vet?" asked Britton.

"A vet is a doctor for animals," said
Dad. "A vet teaches us how to take
care of our pet."

Britton and Dad took the kitten to the vet. Dr. Marcus checked her eyes and ears. She listened to the kitten's heart. She opened the kitten's mouth and looked at her teeth.

"Your cat is very healthy," Dr. Marcus said. "She has the features of a calico cat."

That night, Britton looked at the new kitten. She was white all over, with orange patches of fur. He named her "Patches."

Patches was shy. At first she was afraid of Britton. She would hide under the kitchen table. She would run away. Later she began to play with him. Soon Patches and Britton were friends.

Patches grew and grew. She was too big for her pillowcase bed. She liked to sleep in Britton's bed. She would curl up by his feet. Sometimes she would wake him up in the morning.

"Meow!" she said.

One day, Britton found scratches on Dad's chair.

"Dad!" called Britton. "Patches is scratching your chair! We need to cut her nails so she cannot scratch."

"We do not need to do that," said Dad. "It's natural for cats to scratch things. We will give her toys that she can scratch."

One day, Britton's teacher said, "We are having show and tell tomorrow."

Britton raised his hand. "I want to show everyone my cat, Patches," Britton said.

Britton's teacher smiled at him.

"That would be fun, Britton," she said. "I would like you to tell us about your cat instead."

At home, Britton thought about his cat. He remembered Patches under the car. He remembered buying her kitten food. He remembered visiting Dr. Marcus. Patches had been afraid of Britton, but now they were friends.

It was time for show and tell.

"Our kitten is named Patches," said Britton. "Before, she was tiny. Now she is bigger. At first, she had a box for a bed. Now she sleeps in my bed. Patches is a great pet!"

Animal Rescuers help care for animals during emergencies, such as earthquakes, floods, or forest fires. People will call a rescuer to remove wild animals, such as bats or squirrels, from their homes.

Animal Rescuers also work with shelters to protect stray cats and dogs that do not have homes.

If you love animals, you might consider working as an Animal Rescuer someday.